ALICE BYRAM
WITH PAULA RINEHART

HEALING
THE BROKEN
PLACES

A WOMEN'S
BIBLE STUDY
FOR DIVORCE
RECOVERY

NAVPRESS
A MINISTRY OF THE NAVIGATORS
P.O. BOX 6000, COLORADO SPRINGS, COLORADO 80934

The Navigators is an international Christian
organization. Jesus Christ gave His followers the
Great Commission to go and make disciples
(Matthew 28:19). The aim of The Navigators is
to help fulfill that commission by multiplying
laborers for Christ in every nation.

NavPress is the publishing ministry of The Navigators. NavPress publications are tools to help
Christians grow. Although publications alone
cannot make disciples or change lives, they can
help believers learn biblical discipleship, and
apply what they learn to their lives and
ministries.

Printed in the United States of America

CONTENTS

AUTHOR

Alice Byram is a divorcée and mother with three children and three living grandchildren. A native Texan, she has worked for The Navigators in the Staff Benefits Department at the International Headquarters in Colorado Springs, Colorado, for twelve years.

While recovering from her own divorce, Alice turned to God for help in her restoration and healing. She soon began developing a heart to help other divorced women work through their devastation and brokenness. Alice has led many small groups and one-on-one Bible studies for women going through divorce.

PREFACE

I stared in disbelief at the papers in my lap as the plane taxied down the runway. Over and over, my eyes returned to the title, "Decree of Divorce." As the plane became airborne, I leaned back in my seat for the flight home. But my thoughts ran rampant.

"I am no longer a married woman." My mind strained to absorb the awesome thought. What had happened?

Images, long forgotten, from the early years of our marriage began to pass before my mind's eye. There were so many happy, exciting times together. I winced with each memory.

If you could have pulled apart the curtains later on, though, and looked inside our home, you would have seen two very busy people, with little communication, constantly surrounded by friends and family. Anger, fear, and disrespect riddled the atmosphere. There were many tears but not much resolution. We had unknowingly opened the door to a thief who was stealthily robbing us of our life together. Divorce was but the final chapter to a story whose plot line should have been rewritten much earlier.

That plane and those papers carried me from Oklahoma to southern Texas where I stepped off into a whole new life as a divorced woman, with three small children in tow. Those were my first steps in the inevitable uprooting and rebuilding process divorce brings, of which this Bible study is one outward expression.

As you and I both know, recovery from divorce isn't accomplished in ten easy steps . . . or eight Bible study chapters either, for that matter. When two people marry, in some mystical way they become one. When divorce occurs, there is a rending, a tearing apart, a pain so physical it seems that others surely must see our open wound. That kind of pain doesn't leave overnight.

But time doesn't heal all wounds either. God does. And He uses His grace and our response in a process that's still something of a mystery to me, though I've watched it with awe, in myself and in others, over the years.

I am convinced that we can't experience the healing and the wholeness we long for apart from the Lord and His Word. It's from this conviction that I encourage you as you begin this study. I hope you will hear God knocking on the door of your life. And I pray that what you may perceive as empty, swept-bare rooms will be filled, once again, to overflowing—with the pleasure of His company.

GETTING THE MOST FROM THIS STUDY

You'll profit most from this study if you're able to take your time as you work on each chapter. You need time to think and reflect, time to pray over the thoughts God brings to mind.

You'll find that the first half of the study is more painful than the last half. Sometimes we have to hurt a bit in order to heal. But the last four chapters will more than make up for the discomfort.

This study is designed to be discussed in a small group or with another individual. There is a particular cathartic relief in sharing our struggles with a small group, or another person who understands.

The journaling exercises included are an integral part of each chapter. They are designed to be done in a separate notebook, one that you can continue adding to later. Even if you've never written down your thoughts in such a manner and you don't think of yourself as a "writer," don't let the exercises intimidate you. You'll be amazed at what flows from the end of your pen. You'll experience unbelievable clarity and resolution as you reread your thoughts later and pray over what you've written.

Finally, you'll find the Bible study you do in these chapters more helpful if you use one of these common translations: the *New International Version* or the *New American Standard Bible.*

1
CONFRONTING THE LOSS

"Divorce is like an automobile demolition derby. Everyone gathers around to watch it. There is a lot of noise while it's going on. When it's finished the last car still running gets the prize. The track is covered with the debris of the other cars, and it takes forever to clean up the mess. The leftover debris can take a lifetime to clean up. The person doing the picking up often wonders and says, 'Is there really life after divorce?'"

JIM SMOKE
Living Beyond Divorce

Divorce is a shattering experience. The image of two cars crashing, scattering debris everywhere, is an accurate description. If you've experienced the disillusionment of divorce—if you're experiencing it even now—you know that few of life's traumas compare to the emotional devastation divorce can bring.

Perhaps there is at least some measure of comfort in knowing that you and I are not alone in our difficulties. Others have shared our feelings. The Bible is a very honest book—a book whose main characters refuse to whitewash the pain and turmoil of their lives. From Job to Jesus Christ, there are no pits of despair lower than those into which they descended. They do not offer us stale clichés from lofty pulpits or other-worldly perches. Rather, from the personal arena of all-too-human struggle, they direct us to the only One who can offer any real and lasting help.

Real Loss . . . Real Pain

Naomi, a great woman of the Old Testament, knew what it was like to experience overwhelming loss. She lived during the difficult period of the judges when famine and hardship were constant companions. As if that was not enough, everything in her life started to disintegrate.

1. Read Ruth 1:1-5. What losses did Naomi experience?

2. You can see the reality of Naomi's struggles with loss by the way she responded to her daughters-in-law and her friends when she returned home.

a. How did she respond to her daughters-in-law? (Ruth 1:8-13).

b. How did she respond to her friends when they greeted her on her return? (Ruth 1:19-21).

3. a. In what way can you identify with Naomi, in any measure, in the loss she experienced?

b. How would you describe your own sense of loss?

4. Thankfully, that's not the end of Naomi's story! (It's not the end of ours, either.) Naomi's daughter-in-law Ruth marries again, completing one of the Bible's greatest love stories. Read Ruth 4:13-17.

a. How would you describe Naomi at the end of the story?

b. How has her life changed?

The Anguish of Regret

Peter was part of the inner circle of men closest to Jesus. From his lips came the first declaration of Christ as the Son of God, the Messiah. Peter was the only disciple to boldly state that he would willingly lay down his life for the Lord (John 13:37).

5. a. Yet somehow Peter failed. When the tide turned against Christ, what was Peter's response? (Luke 22:54-60).

b. How did Peter feel? (Luke 22:61-62).

6. All marriages, even those that remain intact, have the problems and deficiencies inevitable in the union of two fallen individuals. We can all look back and think of things we wish we'd done differently. In what ways, if any, have you shared the anguish of regret Peter expresses in this passage?

7. Peter's failure was not the end of his story. The following passage in Acts reveals a man who had profited from failure. Read Acts 5:27-32,40-42. How would you describe Peter now?

When No One Understands

David's life was full of painful experiences. He spent years on the run from Saul, hiding out in caves and dodging spears, until the time when God would make him king. Then, after all God had done for him, he committed adultery with Bathsheba. Though he fasted and prayed, their first son died.

8. a. Many of the psalms record David's sense of being alone in his misery. From these verses, how would you describe the way David felt?

Psalm 69:20

Psalm 142:4

b. Have you ever felt that no one could really understand what you were going through? If so, in what
ways have you felt that?

A Ray of Hope

For any of us who have been through the pain of divorce,
we know there are no quick fixes, no Band-Aid solutions
to the anguish we've experienced. And yet there is reason for hope. The lives of Naomi and Peter and David all
illustrate this simple, profound truth: Only God can
mend a broken heart.

The expression of this hope is most eloquently
stated by David. His psalms are windows into his soul.
When we read them we see not only his turmoil and
despair, but also his hope that God would bring him
through.

9. As you look through these windows, what do you
see? What did David ask of the Lord? What did He
believe God would do for Him?

How David felt	What David did	What he believed God would do for him
Psalm 31:19-22		

How David felt	What David did	What he believed God would do for him
Psalm 42:3-8		
Psalm 142:5-7		

10. a. David's hope could be summarized by his statements in Psalm 40:1-3. Read this passage and describe the process of spiritual and emotional restoration David went through.

b. What hope does the change in David's outlook give to you?

11. The Lord spoke words of encouragement to His people in their captivity. Read Jeremiah 29:11-13. What kind of outlook on the future does God want us to have?

Having Been There Myself

Certain memories stand out in my mind from the early days following my divorce. I recall only too well what it's like to be jarred awake in the morning as you reach over to touch someone and realize . . . he isn't there. I know how panic steals in when your car breaks down in rush-hour traffic . . . and you have no one to call.

There were plenty of daily reminders of my husband's absence, but even more, I felt God had abandoned me, too. I knew God had created marriage to be a lifelong relationship between two people, and my marriage had failed. I had failed. I felt alone in the universe.

So I did what many people do when they feel terribly alone. I filled my life with activities and work and people—anything to keep from being by myself, from being reminded of the pain. (Others retreat into isolation, too depressed and unmotivated to venture forth.) I turned away from God; after all, He seemed to have turned away from me. I ran the other way until I was too exhausted to take another step.

When I finally stopped running, I discovered a comforting fact. God had been there all along . . . waiting for me to bring Him the broken pieces of my life and let Him put me back together, His way.

As you come to the close of this first chapter, take a few moments to review what you've observed in the lives of Naomi, Peter, and David. Perhaps this is the time for you to ask the Lord to give you a new sense of His presence with you in what may seem some of the most difficult circumstances you've ever encountered.

The LORD is close to the brokenhearted and
saves those who are crushed in spirit.
Psalm 34:18

2
MOVING BEYOND REJECTION

"Rejection has to do with personal devaluation. . . . The hurt may not come out in so many words. In fact, your spouse might be very civil about the whole thing. But by divorcing you, your spouse seems to be saying, 'You're worthless.' 'Whatever you once had, you've lost it.' 'I have better things to do with my life than spend it with you.'"

ANDRÉ BUSTANOBY
But I Didn't Want a Divorce

Wedding days provide a lifelong collection of memories. A nervous groom in a fresh tuxedo. The sweet smell of flowers. The ever-present flashes of some uncle's camera. Warm, lighthearted hugs on a day too warm already.

Yet somewhere between lighting the candles and eating the wedding cake, words were exchanged—the simple, clear words, "I do." I do take you to be my wife. And I take you to be my husband. I desire you above all others. I choose to live out my days with you.

How did this perfect, picturesque day give way to cold shoulders and broken promises? "I do take you" became, "I have better things to do than spend my life with you." Experiencing the rejection of someone you have loved is the painful reversal of all your happiest memories. There is no greater sense of feeling unwanted.

Once again, the Bible speaks to us from the lips of people who've lived through the pain of rejection. What can you and I learn from them? What can we learn about God's response to their pain . . . and ours?

Our Most Natural Response

Rejection can be so painful that sometimes our first inclination is to run from the circumstances and isolate ourselves.

Hagar, who was the maid of Abraham's wife, Sarah, was able to conceive the child that Sarah, herself, longed to have. Consequently, Sarah treated her harshly. Read Genesis 16:6-13 to see what happened to Hagar.

1. How do you think Hagar must have felt when she realized she was alone in the wilderness, isolated from everyone?

22

2. a. In verse 13, Hagar reveals what she learned about the Lord. What name did she call the Lord?

b. What do you think she was saying about God?

Someone Who Understands

Even Jesus—especially Jesus—was no stranger to the pain of rejection. He knew rejection from the day of His birth until the day He died.

3. Read Isaiah's often-quoted verse about Christ (53:3). What various facets of the rejection Jesus experienced can you identify in this verse?

4. Christ did not experience rejection in some detached way, as though He was separated from the pain by an invisible, protective shield. On His way to Jerusalem to die, Jesus cries out in strong, anguished grief. Read Luke 13:34 and describe the reason for that grief and frustration.

5. As Christ endured rejection, what comforted Him? (John 16:32).

6. Do you think God can understand, even empathize
with, rejection you've felt? What comfort do you
draw from the insight these two verses give?

Isaiah 63:9

Hebrews 7:25

Coming Home

We have no greater need than to know, in a deep, solid
sense, that we are loved and accepted by God. Through
the pages of sixty-six different books, in the agony of a
wooden cross, God has gone to great lengths to com-
municate that He loves us.

C.S. Lewis once said, "God whispers to us in our
pleasures, speaks in our conscience, but shouts in our
pain: It is His megaphone to rouse a deaf world."[1]

7. Through our pain we need to let God speak. What do these verses say about His love and care for you?

Psalm 72:12

Isaiah 40:11

Isaiah 49:15-16

And yet it's not enough to read verses that remind us of God's love for us. At some point, we need to *receive* His love. Take a few moments to pray:

▶Describe the way you feel to the Lord and why;
▶Thank Him that His love for you is so solid and lasting that no person's response can permanently disable you;
▶Ask Him to make that love real to you in a daily, experiential way.

You may want to take a verse from this study that is meaningful to you personally, copy it on an index card, and put the card in a prominent place for easier recall.

Having Been There Myself

Perhaps the most devastating words anyone ever hears are these: "I don't love you anymore." Certainly that was the case for me. The bottom of life seemed to drop out from under me and for a while, I couldn't grab hold of anything that made life worth living.

Many times, at this point of vulnerability, we're tempted to rebound right into a relationship with another man. We need a hand to hold . . . someone there whose face helps to erase the images of pain or rejection still so fresh in our mind. Maybe this is why such a high percentage of second marriages fail: There is so much rebuilding needed in one person's life before he or she can share life again with someone else.

In my own life, I began, little by little, to take comfort in the realization that God would never say those words, "I don't love you anymore," to me. The rejection I had experienced came to be the black backdrop against which the love of God shone in singular brilliance. One verse came back to my mind over and over again. God's promise to each of us is in His Word: "I will never desert you, nor will I ever forsake you" (Hebrews 13:5, NASB).

> *"The LORD your God goes with you; he will*
> *never leave you nor forsake you."*
> Deuteronomy 31:6

NOTE: 1. C.S. Lewis, *The Problem of Pain* (New York: Macmillan Publishing Co., 1962), page 93.

3
SMOLDERING EMBERS

"You get furious and blow up. The target [your ex-husband] is easy to mark. The deep anger you feel over the loss of your basic life's dream and the shortening of your value system is directed at your former spouse. Like burn victims, separating spouses usually cannot even breathe on each other without precipitating a crisis. Hell hath no fury like two people who have separated."

ABIGAIL TRAFFORD
Crazy Time: Surviving Divorce

Of all the emotions that accompany the pain of a broken relationship, anger is perhaps the most difficult to handle. Icy glares, menacing threats, hot and angry accusations, slamming doors—the sights and sounds of a marriage coming apart are not pleasant. Seldom do we part in peace.

Most of us are left with the residue of that anger. Before the audiences of our lives—our children, our families, our colleagues—we may be able to present an image of even-tempered calm. But underneath the placid surface, often the anger still smolders, threatening to consume us if we are once caught off guard.

Anger, a Festering Sore

Each of us set out upon the course of marriage with high hopes. We longed for the warmth and intimacy of a close, committed relationship. Experiencing the wilderness of divorce was not what we had in mind.

The children of Israel felt much the same way once they'd left Egypt en route to the Promised Land. The journey was not at all what they'd envisioned.

1. Read Numbers 20:1-5 and notice the anguish in the Israelites' words.

a. What were their complaints?

b. Why were they so frustrated?

2. How has your experience of divorce been the disappointment of your former hopes?

How We Respond

3. Adam and Eve model the most natural of human responses when something goes wrong. What is that response? (Genesis 3:9-13).

Eventually our disappointed hopes give way to anger and frustration. "It's not fair," we find ourselves thinking. "No one should have to live like this."

And in some measure, that's true. The pain of broken relationships is part of living in a fallen world with fallen individuals, and in that sense, we are angry at what grieves and angers God as well. The emotion of anger is part of being human; it's what we do in response to that emotion that's most important.

We may have one of two common responses to anger. We may refuse to admit its presence, ashamed to acknowledge what seem like "unspiritual" feelings. Or we may actually nurse the anger we know is there. Either way, the results of not dealing with our anger can be disastrous because anger that is allowed to build up becomes *resentment* and *bitterness*.

Thinking on Paper: An Exercise in Journaling
When you're really honest with yourself, what emotions surface? Are you angry? Anger is a natural response to rejection and loss, but it's also a signal to alert us to even deeper issues we need to work through, like blaming and resentment.

When we hold resentment toward someone, we give that person a certain measure of control over us. Our resentment holds us captive to a rigid way of feeling and responding. Our journey out of the tunnel of anger begins with admitting our anger exists. The next crucial step is identifying the part we are playing in keeping the resentment alive. When we take responsibility for that, we're half the way home.

Try to fill in the following sentence: "I am angry at . . . because . . . ." Be as specific and as thorough as you can, and keep writing until you have covered every person you can think of. Then answer the following questions:

Where has my desire for self-esteem and security been threatened?

What goals and ambitions have been thwarted?

What fears are beneath my anger?

In what ways is my anger based on self-centeredness?

What does my anger tell me about myself?

4. The Apostle Paul wrote about the emotion of anger in Ephesians 4:26-27. What cautions did he include?

30

5. Anger that becomes bitterness will not long remain a personal, private struggle. What are some of the effects of nursing our anger?

Hebrews 3:13

Hebrews 12:15

Because the prolonged effects of anger can be so devastating, Paul tells the Ephesians, "Let all bitterness and wrath and anger and clamor and slander be put away from you, along with all malice" (Ephesians 4:31, NASB).

6. Anger can assume many forms. Paul mentions some of those: bitterness, wrath, clamor, slander, and malice. Look at the meaning of these words in a good dictionary. What insight do you gain into the broader meaning of anger?

7. a. When you and I allow God to help us deal with the anger in our lives, what kinds of attitudes and actions begin to change?

   b. What spiritual dynamic takes place in the life of a person who begins to deal with his or her anger? (1 Peter 2:1-2).

Resting Our Case

As Job faced some of the most difficult circumstances ever recorded in Scripture, he found himself, at times, frustrated and angry. He presented his case before God. What God gave Job was not so much "answers" to his questions as it was a fresh realization of Himself.

8. Read Job 42:1-6. What had Job learned about God that helped him release his anger and frustration?

9. a. Perhaps much of Job's progress was the result of his willingness to take his frustration to the Lord. Why is this usually so difficult for us to do?

   b. What insight do you gain from these verses that might make it easier for you to acknowledge your struggles to the Lord?

   Psalm 38:9

   Hebrews 4:13-16

10. a. As Job's example illustrates, only a renewed sense of the greatness of God will enable us to rest our case with Him. Look at Romans 11:33-36. What aspects of the nature of God are mentioned here?

   b. How does our understanding of God's nature increase our trust and confidence to go to Him with negative emotions?

Having Been There Myself

My divorce took place many years ago, during a time when divorce was far from commonplace. Neither divorce nor its accompanying emotions—anger, bitterness, resentment—were acknowledged or addressed in Christian circles.

At a quick glance, I appeared to have handled well the difficulties inherent in divorce. For the most part, though, I had merely pressed a smile on my face and stuffed my anger and resentment out of sight. I hid my anger successfully (most of the time) from myself, from God, and from everyone else. But deep down, underneath the placid facade, I was asking myself how God could have let this happen.

Slowly the anger began to surface in rather obvious ways. The little things, as well as the big things, upset me. I was a working mother with three small children, and I didn't want that responsibility. I found myself resenting the amount of time it took to be a single parent. I was overwhelmed.

Strangely enough, being willing to admit how very angry I was became the first step toward making real progress. I had to admit that I was in the tunnel before I could come out on the other side. Only then could God's cleansing, healing process begin.

The next chapter is actually a continuation of this one. It will serve to clarify and resolve more of this issue of dealing effectively with the anger that inevitably arises in divorce.

Why do you say, O Jacob, and assert,
O Israel, "My way is hidden from the LORD,
and the justice due me escapes
the notice of my God"?
Isaiah 40:27, NASB

4

THE IMPOSSIBLE NECESSITY

"For here and now, the unforgiven and unforgiving person is plagued with guilt and resentment. He lives in a prison house where he finds himself tortured by all manner of inner emotional conflicts."

DAVID SEAMANDS
Healing for Damaged Emotions

Once the initial chaotic storms of divorce subside, with hard work and stern resolve it's possible to carry on in life with some degree of normalcy. Somehow bills get paid, the children's homework gets done—life once again takes on the steady rhythm of routine. On the surface, we seem to be doing better.

Yet we long for more than superficial gains. At this point on our road to recovery many of us face our greatest challenge: to forgive those who have wronged us and to accept God's forgiveness for ourselves. Herein lies the key to the healing and wholeness we desire.

Forgiveness in the face of deep hurt requires the supernatural power and grace of God. Yet as we turn to the Bible we find that indeed God has been in the business of forgiveness from the beginning of time.

Weighing Debts

Jesus used the story of a king and his servant to illustrate how God forgives and how He requires that we forgive as well. Read Matthew 18:21-35 several times, in different translations if possible. Take some time to imagine the three mini-scenes that take place in this passage:

▶The king and his wayward servant
▶The servant and his delinquent friend
▶Once again, the king and his wayward servant

The servant owed the king the sum of 10,000 talents, which would be millions of dollars in today's United States currency. The servant's friend, on the other hand, owed him only 100 denarii, equal to a few of our dollars.[1]

1. What is the spiritual parallel being illustrated by the wide variance in these two sums?

2. a. How did the forgiven servant respond to his friend's debt?

b. If that same servant had rightly appreciated the debt forgiven him by the king, what would the servant's response have been to the debt that was owed him?

3. a. Look back at verses 21 and 22. When Peter suggested that we ought to forgive seven times, he felt he was being magnanimous (since Jewish teaching required only three). What was Jesus' response to Peter's question?

b. From the insight you've gained in this parable, why do you think Jesus exacted the higher standard?

4. a. The teaching of this parable could be summarized by one clear, concise verse: Ephesians 4:32. As you read this verse and think back over the par-

37

able, what basis can you see for forgiving those who have wronged you?

b. What does Jesus say is the danger of not forgiving those who have wronged us? (Matthew 6:14-15).

Jesus, The Wounded Healer

No one has endured more harm at the hands of others than Jesus Christ. He was misunderstood, mocked, and betrayed. Even His closest friends turned against Him. Yet, on the cross He uttered those amazing words, "Father, forgive them."

5. How is His example meant to encourage us? (Hebrews 12:3).

6. In the face of the difficult task of forgiving, we need more than Christ's example. We need His power. Read Ephesians 1:18-23 and consider this question: What is the nature of the power God makes available to you and me in Christ?

7. If forgiving those who have wronged us is both necessary and yet beyond our human ability to accomplish, how then can we hope to forgive? (1 Peter 1:21-23).

Some Practical Helps Toward Forgiveness

Real forgiveness never comes easily, yet it offers the only hope for being able to move forward in life, free of the past. If you've come to that realization, you might find that you're able to experience that release in one or more of the following ways:

A Letter Written but Not Mailed

If you can, write a letter to your ex-husband (or whoever you feel has wronged you) and include elements such as these:

> ▶your positive memories of him
> ▶your negative memories of him and of your relationship, and how those things made you feel
> ▶what you want to be freed from (e.g., anger, expectations, pain)
> ▶your willingness to forgive
> ▶what decisions you are making on how you're going to think and live from now on
> ▶what kind of relationship you're now going to have with him

Praying Through Forgiveness Personally

This is a matter of taking some concentrated time with the Lord to pour out your heart honestly before Him, asking Him to bring back to your mind memories that illustrate what you need to forgive and the resentment you've harbored, and then voicing your willingness to forgive through Christ.

Specific Prayer with a Trusted Friend

Sometimes it helps to pray through the difficult issue of forgiveness with another person who can pray for you as you pray and who can support you as you cross this most difficult of hurdles.

You may not be able to take this step of forgiving yet at this point. If not, then openly acknowledge that to the Lord. Even if you can only honestly say, "Lord, I am willing to be made willing to forgive," you'll find God will meet you right where you are and give you the grace to move forward . . . one step at a time.

Experiencing God's Forgiveness

It's not just "the other person" who needs to be forgiven. In any relationship, no one person is entirely blameless—no one entirely guilty. We need to know God's forgiveness ourselves. We need to experience the freedom of being released from the mistakes of our past.

8. How does David describe the effects of refusing to admit guilt? (Psalm 32:3-4).

9. God offers us not a cheap but a very costly forgiveness. The barrier between us and God could be removed only through the death of His Son. "In him we have redemption through his blood, the forgiveness of sins, in accordance with the riches of God's grace that he lavished on us with all wisdom and understanding" (Ephesians 1:7-8).

Because of the sacrifice of Christ, *to what extent* is God willing to forgive us?

Psalm 103:10-13

Isaiah 43:25

10. It is at this wonder—that a holy, righteous God could completely forgive—that the prophet Micah marvels in the closing section of his book. Read what he says about the forgiving grace of God in Micah 7:18-19. How would you put those thoughts in your own words?

Thinking on Paper: An Exercise in Journaling
Think through some of your memories of the past. Write about the ones that plague you most. Which mistakes do you most wish you could erase?

Now as you write, focus in on this question: How would God respond to what you have written? Spend some time praying through what you have on paper. Are you able to receive His forgiveness? Why or why not?

Forgiving and being forgiven are, by nature, intertwined. We are able to forgive as we are forgiven. As we experience God's forgiveness, we can more easily extend it to others.

> "To forgive is to set a prisoner free and discover that the prisoner was you."
>
> Lewis Smedes,
> *Forgive and Forget*

41

Having Been There Myself

I know only too well how difficult it is to associate the word *forgiveness* with the word *divorce*. The hurts are too deep, the pain too real. The prospect of forgiving my ex-husband, of forgiving myself, was like a rugged mountain I carefully surveyed . . . but then repeatedly turned and walked away from.

You and I are accustomed to overlooking annoyances. We know what it is to brush off minor irritations. But betrayal, injustice, sin—these are the heavy-duty issues I soon saw were possible to forgive only by the grace of God. It came as no small comfort to me to realize that forgiveness is *His* area of expertise.

About this time, a familiar verse in Philippians became very relevant to me: "I can do everything through him who gives me strength" (Philippians 4:13). God could give me the strength to forgive those I felt had wronged me, and even more, to forgive myself. I knew there were ways in which I'd failed as well.

There was a point at which I voiced to God in a deliberate way, "Lord, by your grace, I do forgive. . . ." And there were many other smaller times when, jarred by an unpleasant memory, I would have to say, "And Lord, I do forgive . . . again." After the initial foundation of forgiveness is laid, we build on it with each memory forgiven . . . one brick at a time. And with each new brick in place we experience a greater measure of freedom and release.

I knew I was making progress when I could pray for God's grace in my ex-husband's life. Slowly, I was being freed from the instant replay of painful memories that left me angry and vengeful. Forgiving and experiencing forgiveness unplugged the videotape from the past and left me much freer to move on in life.

As the anger, bitterness, and resentment began to seep out of my life, a much greater desire for a close relationship with the Lord began to take hold. The Bible became a book that was alive and full of meaning. Here was the God of the universe, and He was seeking me!

42

I was hearing His voice more clearly than I had for a
long, long time.

"So let us know, let us press on to know the LORD.
His going forth is as certain as the dawn;
And He will come to us like the rain,
Like the spring rain watering the earth."
Hosea 6:3, NASB

NOTE: 1. *The NIV Study Bible,* Kenneth Barker ed. (Grand Rapids: Zondervan
Publishing Co., 1985), page 1469.

5
HALF IS STILL WHOLE

"No matter when a marriage breaks up, divorce can be devastating because of the feeling of failure it typically calls up. Many people look upon marriage as the single most important relationship of their lives, and when that relationship breaks up, they feel like complete and utter failures. Usually in the wake of divorce the loss of self-esteem is only temporary, but that still doesn't make it easy to handle."

LINDA TSCHIRHART SANFORD and MARY ELLEN DONOVAN
Women & Self-Esteem

In the great puzzle of life, where do we, as divorced women, fit? For years we have thought of ourselves as wives, as spouses, as one half of the whole our culture calls "couple." Now old foursomes have become awkward triangles. The Internal Revenue Service lists "Head of Household" beside our names. We're no longer sure who we are or where we belong. Our worth is decidedly undetermined.

Our only hope of coming to grips with who we are and where we fit requires a regression of sorts . . . a going back to the time when the words *marriage* and *divorce, single* and *couple* were not in our vocabulary. The dilemma of establishing a sense of personal worth must always take place at a more fundamental level: between God and us alone.

Long before you and I belonged to another person, we belonged to God.[1] We are His idea. Our worth in God's eyes is best understood in the cold, hard silhouette of a cross set against a Mideastern skyline. This is the place we need to start if we want to establish a strong, unassailable foundation for our personal worth.

But here . . . let God speak for Himself.

The Great Designer

1. You and I may have only recently turned to God. But there has been nothing "recent" about His turning toward us. Read in Psalm 139:13-16 a clear witness to God's longstanding concern for you.

What insights do you gain from these verses about God's involvement in your life?

2. In Isaiah, the Lord speaks strong and comforting words to Israel. You and I are likewise, because of Christ, considered part of God's special people (Romans 9:6-8). Read Isaiah 43:1-2.

a. What is the strong message to you and me?

b. What are those comforting words?

3. What do these two verses tell you about the sense of belonging and acceptance that God offers each of us in Christ?

John 15:15

Ephesians 1:4-6

4. How would you summarize what you've discovered so far about your value to God?

His Limitless Love

5. Take a few moments to read through, two or three times, one of the most radiant passages on the love of God: Romans 8:28-39.

  a. List as many ways in which God demonstrates His love for us as you can find in this passage.

  b. Which is the most encouraging to you? Why?

6. It's perhaps the supreme irony that though God has gone to such lengths to demonstrate His love for us and our worth to Him, we so often turn in every other direction but to Him to have our needs met.

God pictures this irony for us in His words to Jeremiah:

> "My people have committed two sins: They have forsaken me, the spring of living water, and have dug their own cisterns, broken cisterns that cannot hold water."
>
> Jeremiah 2:13

  a. How does God describe Himself in this verse?

b. And how does He picture the futility of looking to anyone or anything other than Him for life and meaning?

c. Why, then, is it impossible to establish a solid sense of identity and worth apart from God?

Thinking on Paper: An Exercise in Journaling
Think back over the course of your life. Take some time to write about what you've relied on in the past to provide you with a sense of personal worth.

One help in discovering this is to think about what you have fought hardest to obtain or feared losing the most.

As you consider what you've relied on in the past, do you have a sense of being disappointed? If so, in what ways?

How has your understanding of an adequate foundation for a sense of personal worth changed as a result of your study?

A Matter of the Heart

We can read verses about the love of God. We can nod our head to the notion that God has made us and redeemed us—we are individuals of value and worth. But, what will move these truths from our head and plant them firmly in our heart? Our response to the Lord is crucial if we want to *experience* His love and the joy of belonging to Him.

7. How does the psalmist describe what it means to seek God? (Psalm 63:1-8).

8. Read that wonderful passage in Jeremiah 29:11-13 again. Think about what it would mean, in your life, for you to seek the Lord "with all your heart." Is there one practical way you can begin, even this week? If so, what?

Having Been There Myself

Living through divorce was the greatest challenge to my sense of personal worth I have ever experienced. Everything I'd previously leaned on had been pulled away, and I felt bare, exposed . . . worthless. Indulging in eating or shopping sprees gave me a temporary lift, but not for long. The despondency, the sense of worthlessness, inevitably returned.

The weeks melted into months, and eventually I found myself back in the psalms, particularly Psalm 139. Though this psalm was familiar, I had never read through these verses as though there was a message there for *me*, for *my* life. As I began to pray through these verses and to absorb the truth that God knew me, that He made me, that He thought of me . . . slowly I began to sense my worth in the eyes of the One whose opinion matters most.

The torn pieces of self-esteem don't magically come back together overnight, like a movie put on rewind. The process of restoration takes time. Yet what's encouraged me most is the realization that God has rebuilt my life on a stronger, more adequate foundation than the one I knew before.

[The Lord said,]
"I have loved you with an everlasting love;
I have drawn you with loving-kindness."
Jeremiah 31:3

NOTE: 1. Though each of us is His creation, let me be sure to clarify that we become His *child* when we individually respond to Him through the death of Christ. He died in our place, and when we place our trust in His finished work on the cross, we enter into a new and vital relationship with God.

This entire Bible study presupposes that you have already personally trusted Christ. But if you haven't, you can respond to Him at any point . . . even now. You have only to admit your need of Him and your understanding of how His death overcame the barrier of your sin, which separated you from God.

This is the basis on which a Bible study, such as this one, can be of real help to you.

6
ON SOLID GROUND

"One of the keys of stabilizing your life is feeling good again about yourself. It is knowing who you are and liking it. It is gaining control from the chaos and establishing priorities and goals. It is having the pieces of the puzzle fit without being forced into place. It is walking on the edge without fear of falling off."

JIM SMOKE
Living Beyond Divorce

When life comes apart at the seams, we're left grasping for something sure and steady. Like children in a rowboat on turbulent seas, we're tossed to and fro by the pressures and upheaval let loose upon our lives. Our emotions can climb to the highest highs and dip just as easily to record lows.

Often, we're left with more questions than answers. Can I ever trust anyone again? Is it possible to find peace in circumstances I wouldn't have chosen? How can I regain my equilibrium?

We long for stability, for that sure, steady sense of knowing it's all right in the center—even when it's all wrong on the edges.

Trying Times

1. In earlier civilizations, cities were protected by a strong, formidable wall around the outside. A city with damaged walls was easily overcome. Thus Proverbs 25:28 (NASB) draws this analogy to our lives: "Like a city that is broken into and without walls is a man who has no control over his spirit."

a. Why is this analogy an appropriate one to describe the person whose mental and emotional state is erratic and unstable?

b. Do you ever feel like "a city that is broken into and without walls"? If so, when?

2. There are some nagging, fundamental questions we're prone to ask in tough situations. Asaph voices these in Psalm 77. Read verses 7-9. How would you summarize, or put into your own words, the questions Asaph asked in his tough circumstances?

The Source of Stability

A Sovereign God
God is not a universe away, watching idly as the sons of men bustle about in this business of keeping the world going.

3. What does the Lord say about His own identity, about His involvement in the universe He created?

Isaiah 41:4

Isaiah 43:10-13

A Solid Rock
Though we often feel alone, cast adrift in that rowboat on a turbulent sea, the Old Testament speaks repeatedly of God as the Rock. He alone is unchanging, trustworthy.

4. a. What insights do you gain from these verses?

Psalm 27:5

Psalm 71:3

Isaiah 44:8

b. Which verse is the most encouraging to you personally? Why?

A Safe Port
Another comforting word-picture used in the Bible to describe God is that of a refuge—a safe port within the storm. As you read the words of these psalmists, consider what they experienced of God.

5. a. How did they view God? What were they confident of?

Psalm 16:8-9

Psalm 91:1-4

b. Reflect again on what David said in Psalm 16:8. What do you think he meant when he said, "I have set the LORD always before me"?

c. How would you or I do that?

6. Take a few moments to summarize what you've learned about God. How can this influence your personal hope for a renewed sense of stability and wholeness?

Thinking on Paper: An Exercise in Journaling

Take a few moments to write about one issue or relationship in your life that is a major cause of concern and instability. What comes to mind? When and why is this a problem?

As you think about this area, write about what you can do to affect the situation and what is beyond your ability to change. Can you identify the specific ways in which you will have to trust God in this matter?

Take some time now to commit this area of concern to the Lord, thanking Him that He has promised to be a solid Rock, a safe Port for you.

Peace of Mind

The life we live outwardly is very much determined by the kinds of thoughts we permit inwardly. You and I are responsible for the mental tapes we allow our minds to play and replay. We can't hope for much peace and stability unless we reexamine and take charge of our *thought life.*

7. Earlier in this study we looked at the mental wrestlings of Asaph in Psalm 77. Turn to that psalm again and read the verses that follow that earlier passage: verses 11 and 12.

a. To what thoughts did Asaph deliberately turn in order to counteract the despondency he felt?

b. What are the "deeds of the LORD" in your life that you can thank Him for?

8. a. The Apostle Paul mentions a list of things we ought to consciously make the effort to center our thoughts upon. What are they? (Philippians 4:8).

b. Now, considering your own thought life, write out one or two areas you would like to see changed. Beside those, write a positive aspect, such as one Paul mentions here, that you could focus on in its place. For example:

A Thought That Wears Me Down	A Deliberate Change in Focus
My son is showing the effects of not having his dad around.	*But one of his uncles is beginning to take some interest in befriending him.*

9. a. The Bible gives two key descriptions of the stable versus the unstable person. Read these two short passages and jot down characteristics of each.

The Stable Person	The Unstable Person
Psalm 1:1-4	
Matthew 7:24-27	

b. From what you observe here, what are some of the spiritual keys to experiencing peace and stability in the midst of upheaval and pressure?

Having Been There Myself

On the other side of divorce, I noticed an unusual phenomenon. After encountering the major calamity of a failed marriage, for some time thereafter I lost my ability to discern between the big problems of life and the small ones. Every bump in the road appeared to me to be a major impasse. I was so fundamentally knocked off balance that I wondered if I would ever again feel strong, secure, stable. I was, indeed, a city with few walls.

Slowly I came to realize that there was a limit to what I could do to change my outward circumstances. The demands of work and mothering were daily realities I could not dismiss lightly. Something had to change, though, and that something was inside of me.

I began to escape—but in a healthy way. I learned what it meant to retreat into the Lord. Reading even familiar verses, like the one that promises that "in all things God works for the good of those who love him, who have been called according to his purpose" (Romans 8:28), became a fresh experience for me. Did I believe, would I believe, that God would use the circumstances of my divorce for my good? The prospect seemed unlikely, but I began to wait with anticipation to see.

The trauma associated with divorce changed my approach to reading the Bible. I had read the Bible off and on all my life. But I found there is a vast difference in knowing the truth and grabbing hold for dear life, a difference that could only be likened to stepping off a cliff into thin air and discovering a Rock, a solid, safe place on which to plant my weary feet.

It's not that I'm never knocked off balance now—quite the contrary. But having experienced God as the Refuge, the Rock the Scriptures speak of so clearly, every pressure, every upheaval becomes a less dreaded occasion. I know what it is to *use* the pressures I encounter as obstacles off which to ricochet into that same quiet place with God where I can receive His strength. I know it's possible to experience stability *in the midst* of trying circumstances.

And He shall be the stability of your times,
a wealth of salvation, wisdom, and
knowledge.
Isaiah 33:6, NASB

7
THE GOD
WHO IS THERE

"What do you do when the TV blows a fuse and you feel like blowing yours? Or when the basement floods and you feel like crying? . . . You may cry because a toilet breaks down or because it snowed heavily and you can't get your car out of the driveway. My divorce left me reeling from all the changes I had to make in my life and all the problems I had to confront. I was scared, lonely; and I had to take care of two young children all by myself. I had little money—no job. What was I to do?"

CATHERINE NAPOLITANE
WITH VICTORIA PELLEGRINO
Living and Loving After Divorce

Most efficient people keep a running "do list" that expands and contracts with accordion-like rhythm. How we await that wonderful moment when we can take out a No. 2 pencil and draw a thick line through item after item after item! Our do-list is shrinking; in fact, for a day or two we can declare ourselves caught up.

Divorced women, especially those with children, rarely have such days. The list of things to do seems never-ending. As soon as you finish balancing your checkbook, you'll go mow the grass. And before you get through with that, your daughter will stop you and ask in her most persuasive voice, "Mom, can't I stay out Friday night, at least one hour later than curfew?" Something or someone is always in need of our attention.

There are many who would offer advice on how to cope. Dozens of women's magazines suggest some way to squeeze more out of a twenty-four-hour day and a mediocre paycheck. Somehow, though, the help we need goes beyond jiffy recipes and tax-sheltered savings.

We need Someone to turn to. Someone in whose presence we can freely say, "Stop. Wait. I'm not superwoman, really I'm not!" We need, in a way we have never needed before, to experience God's help—His provision, His wisdom, and His strength.

A God Who Provides

In a familiar portion of the Sermon on the Mount, Jesus refers to God repeatedly as "your heavenly Father." And what does a good Father do? He provides for His children.

1. Read and consider carefully Matthew 6:25-34. You might want to read it through a couple of times, noting the imagery as well as the instruction.

a. Jesus mentions a number of reasons *why* we can and should relax in God's promise to provide for our material needs. What are those reasons?

64

Verse 26

Verse 27

Verse 30

Verse 32

b. In verse 33, Jesus tells us that God will provide
our material needs while we freely devote our
emotional energy to two things. What are they
and how would you define each of them?

c. In verse 34, Jesus does not tell us to refrain from
planning toward the future. What *does* He specifi-
cally tell us not to do, and why?

2. a. What does God promise concerning His willingness and ability to provide for us?

Psalm 34:10

Psalm 138:6-8

b. Do you see any conditional statements inter-
woven in the promises of these verses?

A God Who Gives Wisdom

Solomon was reported to be the wisest man who ever
lived. Yet in the preface of his request to the Lord for *His*
wisdom, Solomon revealed a deep sense of personal
inadequacy. He makes this interesting statement: "O
LORD my God . . . I am only a little child and do not
know how to carry out my duties" (1 Kings 3:7).
Solomon was wise enough to know he needed more
than his own wisdom.

The Bible reserves the harshest condemnation for
the self-sufficient person who thinks that somehow a tad
of common sense, a bit of woman's intuition, even a
heavy dose of intellectual prowess will see her through.

3. What are the characteristics of the person content to
rely on her own wisdom, and what are the results of
that delusion?

The characteristics	The results
Proverbs 16:25	
Proverbs 26:12	
Isaiah 47:10-11	

4. a. What did David cry out to the Lord in Psalm 61:2?

b. What kind of perspective did David allude to when he used the imagery of a "rock that is *higher*" than he was?

5. The cornerstone of experiencing God's wisdom in our lives is knowing the *truth*. "Your word is truth," Jesus said (John 17:17). What does God promise as we begin to establish our lives upon the truth of His Word?

Psalm 51:6

John 8:31-32

6. We can be encouraged that God wants to give us His wisdom as much as we long to receive it. If we lack wisdom we only have to ask a God who gives generously and without reproach (James 1:5).

In the following verses, how is the attitude of seeking God's wisdom described?

Psalm 143:8

Proverbs 3:5-7

7. What steps are you taking or do you intend to take in order to build your life on the truth of God's Word?

A God Who Gives Strength

Amidst the pressured demands of single living, we especially need God's strength. There is just not enough of "us" to go around.

8. Isaiah speaks to our need. He speaks of the awesome grandeur of the God who numbers the stars and shapes the mountains. Read Isaiah 40:25-31 thoughtfully.

a. What does verse 26 say about how God deals with the stars He created?

b. Why is this such an appropriate introduction to the remaining verses about God's strength and care?

c. What characteristics of God do you see in this passage? (See especially verses 28 and 29.)

d. Isaiah says that the person who waits on God will gain new strength. How would you complete this sentence: For me to wait on God would mean . . .

e. Experiencing God's strength is characterized in three ways in verse 31. What phrases describe these three kinds of strength?

9. In some cases, just to be able to *walk* through a difficult time and not grow weary is a valid expression of experiencing supernatural strength. Is there any situation in your life recently in which, with God's help, you were able to "walk and not be faint"?

10. From the following verses, what insight and encouragement do you gain concerning God's strength?

Psalm 50:15

Psalm 68:19

Psalm 119:32

Thinking on Paper: An Exercise in Journaling
When you think about your own personal needs or those of your family, what needs come to mind? Take some time to write about them, and ask yourself, "Which needs are the most crucial? How specific have I been in voicing those requests to the Lord?"

Take some time to write out a prayer asking God to demonstrate His faithfulness to you in some particular areas of your life, so you can grow in your ability to believe God for His help in your circumstances.

Having Been There Myself

I stepped out of the doctor's office into the bright glare of Colorado sunshine. Once inside my car I sat and stared out onto a sea of parked cars, thinking over what he'd said. "You are worn out, Alice," he'd told me. "What you need is three weeks in Hawaii sitting on the beach, with nothing to do but bury your toes in warm sand."

And then we'd both laughed. But on the inside I was closer to tears than laughter. What a preposterous idea to think that I could put together the time and money to take an extended vacation!

As I returned home from the doctor's office that day, I knew that vacation or not, I was going to have to make some changes. My children were now teenagers and there was hardly anything they hadn't tried, at least once. I was worn out from trying to bear the weight of my own struggles and theirs, too.

The longer I thought and prayed, the more I realized why I was so tired. I'd been on that old treadmill again with a fifty-pound weight strapped to my back and an image of me-against-the-world etched in my brain. Once again, I'd run out ahead of the Lord.

It's hard to experience His strength in your weakness if your weakness is the very thing you're most determined to hide. Yet in this instance, as in many others, I have slowly come to see my weakness as a friend. Only from this posture can I experience the reality of the rest and strength that God alone does give. As Jesus said:

"Come to me, all you who are weary and
burdened, and I will give you rest. Take my
yoke upon you and learn from me, for I am
gentle and humble in heart, and you will
find rest for your souls. For my yoke is easy
and my burden is light."
Matthew 11:28-30

8
LOOKING FORWARD TO LIFE

"Human pain does not let go of its grip at one point in time. . . . There is a season of sadness, a season of anger, a season of tranquility, a season of hope. But seasons do not follow one another in a lockstep manner. . . . The winters and springs of one's life are all jumbled together in a puzzling array. . . . But when one affirms that the spring thaw will arrive, the winter winds seem to lose some of their punch."

ROBERT VENINGA
A Gift of Hope

An assortment of trite and trivial expressions sur-
round the subject of hope. There are rainbows
with pots of gold and clouds with silver linings
and tunnels with light at the end. Such is the stuff of fairy
tales, where a knight in shining armor always rescues a
damsel in distress.

But where do you find hope in the real world of
mortgage payments and lonely nights? Is there a way to
stare in the face of the future without cringing?

One of the closing comments in the book of
Romans begins this way: "May *the God of hope* fill you
with all joy and peace as you trust in him" (Romans
15:13). Jesus is not just a sugarcoating for life's bitter
pills. He is the God of hope because He alone can bring
gain from loss. He brings hope for the future.

A Reason for Hope

Joseph was sold into slavery by his own brothers. He
spent years languishing in a prison cell because of a
seductive woman's lie. Yet somehow he saw God's hand
outlining the edges of his experience, and that alone
gave him hope.

1. Read the fascinating account in Genesis 50:15-21 of
Joseph's encounter with his brothers years after their
betrayal of him.

How did Joseph see the hand of God on his life
in overcoming the injustice of his circumstances?

2. Moses, likewise, gave the children of Israel some
insight into how God dealt with them in the wilder-

ness. What reasons can you discover about *why* God allows hard times in our lives? (Deuteronomy 8:10-18).

3. The only accurate cause for hopelessness, then, is a human one. If we turn away from God, dig in our heels, and try to manage on our own—then we have just cause for despair. "Only the rebellious," the psalmist says, "dwell in a parched land" (Psalm 68:6, NASB).

What happens in our lives when we do turn aside from God?

1 Samuel 12:21

2 Chronicles 12:14

A Fresh Start

Precisely because there *is* hope, it makes a difference whether we choose to live for the Lord or not. Now is the time to start clean.

4. As you make a new start in life, and possibly even in your relationship with the Lord, what instruction and encouragement do these verses provide?

Instruction	Encouragement
Deuteronomy 30:19-20	
Isaiah 43:18-19	

5. a. Read and consider Ephesians 4:17-22. How would you describe the way of thinking and the kind of life that you and I, as Christians, have turned from?

b. What kind of life is God calling us to? (Ephesians 4:1-2,23-24).

6. Take a few moments to summarize what you've concluded thus far about a solid basis for hope.

Thinking on Paper: An Exercise in Journaling

In what ways have you sensed that you're making a fresh start in life? In what areas of your life are you beginning to see hope where before the shades were all gray or black?

Take a few minutes to write about the corners God has helped and is helping you to turn. Are there any steps to make or obstacles to overcome that still seem impossible . . . hopeless? How do you think the Lord would respond to what you've written?

A Confident Expectation

When we've given up on everything but the Lord, there is a patient but eager expectancy for the future that slowly begins to take root in our lives.

7. Consider Paul's outlook on life in Philippians 3:12-14.

a. What attitude toward the past and the future is expressed here?

b. For what might God have laid hold of you?

8. The following verses offer encouraging possibilities for the person who has allowed God to shepherd her through difficult times. What are those possibilities?

Psalm 73:28

2 Corinthians 1:3-5

9. How do you and I *know*, even from this small sampling of verses, that God is good and that we'll experience His goodness as we walk with Him?

Psalm 31:19

Isaiah 30:18

Having Been There Myself

Divorce has been described as a major amputation; certainly the pain involved is comparable. But in God's grace and timing, there is healing for the hurt. Life does begin again.

I have always loved a statement Benjamin De Casseres once made: "Hope is the gay, skylarking pajamas we wear over yesterday's bruises." It is a rather poetic way of saying, yes, the situation has been undeniably painful. Yet in the place of that pain I see evidence of hope and healing. In fact, because of all I've seen God do in my life as a result, even the pain has become something of a gift.

God indeed brings gain from loss, and we can't hope to receive what we really long for by searching in any other direction. No, the solution to my problems is not another man. Life isn't going to be all sweetness and light when I finally get that promotion at work. A biblical sense of hope is what you and I grab hold of when we've finally exhausted our illusions.

I know that eight Bible study lessons are only enough to make a solid start—one that you and the Lord will continue to build on for a long time to come. Sometimes the progress you make feels like it's three steps forward and two steps back. But it is progress, and I too have to remind myself of that every so often. The point of real encouragement comes when you begin to see God use your experience as an instrument of His healing in the lives of others.

I would have despaired unless I had believed
that I would see the goodness of the LORD
in the land of the living. Wait for the LORD;
be strong, and let your heart take courage;
yes, wait for the LORD.
Psalm 27:13-14, NASB

SUGGESTED READING

Allen, Charles L. *When a Marriage Ends.* Old Tappan, New Jersey: Fleming H. Revell Company, 1986.

Billheimer, Paul E. *Don't Waste Your Sorrows.* Minneapolis, Minnesota: Bethany House Publishers, 1977.

Birkey, Verna. *You Are Very Special.* Old Tappan, New Jersey: Fleming H. Revell Company, 1977.

Brogan, John P., and Ula Maiden. *The Kid's Guide to Divorce.* New York: Fawcett Crest Books, 1986.

Bustanoby, André. *But I Didn't Want a Divorce.* Grand Rapids, Michigan: Zondervan Publishing House, 1978.

Caldwell, Genevieve. *First Person, Singular.* Nashville, Tennessee: Thomas Nelson, Inc., 1986.

Crabb, Lawrence J. *Understanding People.* Grand Rapids, Michigan: Zondervan Publishing House, 1987.

Galloway, Dale E. *Dream a New Dream.* Wheaton, Illinois: Tyndale House Publishers, Inc., 1975.

Gardner, Richard A. *The Parent's Book About Divorce.* New York: Bantam Books, 1977.

Hershey, Terry. *Beginning Again.* Laguna Hills, California: Merit Books, 1984.

Le Shan, Eda. *What's Going to Happen to Me?* New York: Aladdin Books, 1978.

Littauer, Florence. *Lives on the Mend.* Waco, Texas: Word Books, 1985.

McDowell, Josh. *His Image . . . My Image.* San Bernardino, California: Here's Life Publishers, Inc., 1984.

Napolitane, Catherine, with Victoria Pellegrino. *Living and Loving After Divorce.* New York: New American Library, 1978.

Powell, John. *Why Am I Afraid to Tell You Who I Am?*
Niles, Illinois: Argus Communications, 1969.

Seamands, David. *Healing for Damaged Emotions.*
Wheaton, Illinois: Victor Books, 1981.

Smoke, Jim. *Growing Through Divorce.* Irvine, California: Harvest House Publishers, 1976.

Smoke, Jim. *Living Beyond Divorce.* Eugene, Oregon:
Harvest House Publishers, 1984.

Solomon, Charles R. *The Ins and Out of Rejection.*
Denver, Colorado: Heritage House Publications,
1976.

Trafford, Abigail. *Crazy Time: Surviving Divorce.* New
York: Harper & Row, Publishers, 1982.

Wagman, Anne. *Successful Single Parenting.* New York:
Meadowbrook, Inc., 1987.

Young, Amy Ross. *By Death or Divorce—It Hurts to
Lose.* Denver, Colorado: Accent Publications, 1976.